STAY WITH ME

Poetry

STACY NICHOLSON

Copyright © 2021 Stacy Nicholson

The moral right of the author has been asserted.

All rights reserved. No part of this publication may be reproduced, stored in or introduced into a retrieval system, or transmitted, in any form, or by any means (electronic, mechanical, photocopying, recording or otherwise) without the prior written consent of the publisher.

Any person who does any unauthorised act in relation to this publication may be liable to criminal prosecution and civil claims for damages.

Images by www.dreamstime.com
Cover and Interior Design by Petya Tsankova

ISBN paperback: 978-0-646-83007-0
ISBN ebook: 978-0-646-83335-4

ACKNOWLEDGMENTS

*Many thanks to my sister Maggie
For helping me to choose a title and a book cover.*

I love you, Maggie!

Stacy Nicholson

**HUNDRED
FACES OF LOVE**

I hope through my love poems that readers experience the feeling of joy and happiness that love brings.

Through my poems which describe pain, I hope to awaken compassion toward people with mental or any other kind of suffering as humans and the parts of society to which we are exposed or by which we are affected.

IN THIS WORLD THERE IS NOTHING MORE BEAUTIFUL THAN LOVE OR MORE VALUABLE THAN THE NOBILITY WHICH A PERSON CAN POSSESS

Stacy Nicholson

CONTENTS

INNOCENT LOVE   1

Dream Catcher	3
Innocent	5
Open Your Heart for Love	7
Take a Chance	9
I Grow for You	11
In Love	13
Love Magic	15
Romance	17
I Belong to You	19
Love Hungry	21
Make me believe in love again	23
Far Away	25

LOVE PAIN   27

Eyes Talk	29
Quote About Heart	30
I Know	31
Betrayed	33
Love Ashes	35
Wounded Bird	37
Price of Love	39

Love River	41
Incapable of Love	43
Quote About Love	44
Disappear with Time	45

LIFE POEMS — 47

The Moment	49
Flower Fields	51
Libero	53
Purple Rose	55
Grown Up	57
Swan	59
Swan 2	61
Lost	63
Life Widow	65
Quote About Fear	66
Black Rose	67
Death	69
Quote About Soul	70
Purgatory	71
Quote About Suffering	72
Suffer	73
Quote About Importance of Faith	74
Survivor	75
Chained	77
Angel Tears	79
Mystic River	81

Somewhere	83
Pray	85
Essence of Life	87
Rain	89
Lion King	91
Hero	93
Queen	95
Children Of God	97

FANTASY POEMS   101

Playful Fairy	103
Modern Fairy Tale	105
Princess from the Dark	107
Power of Heart	109
Warrior Princess	111
Multiplied	113

WOMAN LOVE   115

Love Intimacy	117
Silence	119
Woman Knows	121
Love Letter	123
Hidden Inside Ocean	125
Life is Not a Cup of Coffee	127
Blue Light Tango	129

Flower	131
Flower 2	133
Sinner	135
In Action	137
Black Love	139
Playful	141
Seduction	143
Domination	145
Only One	147
Love Enchantment	149
Lust Desire	151
Sex Desire	153
Man Power	155
Black Storm	157
Meet Me	159
Star Dust	161
Angel Mine	163
What a Woman Wants	165
One With Wings	167
Love?	169
What I believe about human existence	171
About the Author	173

INNOCENT LOVE

INNOCENT LOVE

DREAM CATCHER

Love is feeling between two hearts
And when two souls whisper to each other.
Love is a sharing of hearts
And when you are ready to die and sacrifice your life
In order to save somebody else.
Love is when you think that you can live and see
Through somebody else's eyes.
Love is when somebody shares with you
Beauty, happiness and pain,
And you are ready to take it all.

Love is the most sacred gift of giving and receiving
With which two people honor each other.

INNOCENT LOVE

INNOCENT

I wonder, if I close my eyes,
Will you kiss me?
I wonder, if I open my heart,
Will you love me?
I wonder, what is love—
Will you show me?
I wonder, if I get lost,
Will you hold my hand?
I wonder, if I give you my soul,
Will you love it?
I wonder
How to show you what I wonder.

INNOCENT LOVE

OPEN FOR LOVE

Wrap me in a net of silk
And light me with thousands of
Shining stars.
Let me be a dream
And live with me.

Open your heart for love and
Make my dream come to life.
Take my hands; magic is real.

Share your love with me.
I will share my stars with you.
Open your heart, and all of this
Is going to come to life.

INNOCENT LOVE

TAKE A CHANCE

I want to walk through a flower garden
you see with your eyes.
I want to be a princess from your dreams.
Your world is beautiful
and I want to be part of it.

My heart is beautiful, too,
and in the middle of paradise
I open the door for you because
I see paradise in you, too.
We are not meant to live alone
or where shadows run free.

I do not care for other people's love.
I want to have love of my own.
I want to know how you will feel
when I surrender in your arms.
I want to know how my heart will beat
when you kiss me.

In my world,
everything is about you and I.

INNOCENT LOVE

I GROW FOR YOU

All my years
I looked for you in flower fields.
I searched for you in my dreams.
I searched for you between the stars.
I hoped to see you each time I closed my eyes.

All my years
I watched for the stars to suck in their light to be ready for a day
When we finally meet so that they might shine for you.
I walked through streets and carried
hope our eyes would finally somewhere accidentally meet.

All my years
I brushed my hair and wanted to make it soft as silk,
To be soft and irresistible for your hands to touch.
I bathed my skin in milk to glow, to be soft,
To be gently irresistible for your kiss.

All my years—until
You find me, make me smile, and take my hand—
I will close my eyes and surrender to you.
You will become my strength, my star, and my heart.
You will give my life purpose and meaning.
We will finally become complete as one.

INNOCENT LOVE

IN LOVE

Take my hand; walk me through flower gardens.
Your love makes me feel like I am a rose.
I want to blend in with all the other roses.

Take my hand; walk me through flower gardens.
Your love gives me wings; I want to fly.
I want butterflies to decorate my hair.

Take my hand; walk me through flower gardens.
I want my bare feet to walk on the soft grass.
Your love makes me alive; I want to enjoy it.

Take my hand; walk me wherever you want.
When I am with you, flower gardens are everywhere.
Take my hand, I will follow you to the end of the world
Because I love you!

INNOCENT LOVE

LOVE MAGIC

Spin the wind around.
Let a burst of colorful, sparkling stars explode from me.
Your eyes make magic when you look at me.

Smile on me.
It is your smile that carries power.
It is your smile that spins my world around.
It is your smile that warms my soul.

Look deep into my eyes and never blink.
Stop the world from spinning, and freeze time.
Let our souls be happy and take the lead.
Let magic live.

INNOCENT LOVE

ROMANCE

My love,
A beautiful dream I am living in and sharing with you—
Dreams where our two hearts belong and love each other.
Our two hearts have finally found each other.

My heart is a beautiful pink rose,
Which you treasure in the middle of your heart.
I am careful not to move because of the magic inside your heart.
I want to stay there forever.

My dream, where I am your glass of wine;
Here in reality, my skin is a blanket of silk wrapped all around you.
While we live our romance,
My moment with you is my with-you forever
Because we belong together.

Our kisses and cuddles
While we make love and nourish each other—
Our romance, our time, ours forever.

INNOCENT LOVE

I BELONG TO YOU

Love me as you never loved anybody before.
Look inside my eyes and see what no one saw before.
Take my hand and walk me along your path of life.
I gift you with myself forever.
Just as my love for you is forever,
Always remember this, and never let go of my hand.

INNOCENT LOVE

LOVE HUNGRY

Love me; in my heart this is only what I want.
Kiss me; it is only what my body desires to feel.
Cuddle me; my heart wants to feel your love.

Give your leaps power to make our souls feel love.
Let your hands explore the beauty of woman in me.
Let your heart enjoy my touch, too.
Bring to life the dreams you have about me.

Do not give me silk and diamonds; what are they for?
I am silk and diamonds in my heart already.
Do not just look at me and tell me you love me.
I am a woman who has desires and dreams about you.

Teach me about life because you know it all.
Show me what love is.
I want to see and feel it all from your heart and eyes.
Love me.
I love you, too, and my heart is open to you.

MAKE ME BELIEVE IN LOVE AGAIN

All my colorful flower fields are drying.
Take my hand and walk me there.
Make it all green and alive again,
For me and for you.

All my beautiful dreams are there.
All my sparks of magic and happiness are there.
I want to feel it again, and I want you to
Feel it with me too.

I will give you my heart for it.
My heart will beat for both of us.
Make magic and bring to life my flower fields again.
My heart makes magic for you.
My heart is yours.

INNOCENT LOVE

FAR AWAY

We are separated, but still you are next to me all the time.
When I close my eyes, I can see you.
When I open my eyes, I feel you next to me again.
My love for you is inside my heart, so you are all the time with me.

No ocean is big enough to separate me from you.
I think about you all the time.
I feel gentleness rule over me.
I am sad sometimes because we are not together.
I even cry because I miss you.

Each of my feelings is shaped by my deep love for you.
And my feelings are ruled by my desire to kiss you,
Cuddle you, and then drown in your arms.

I am imagining all the time the reflection in your eyes when
They showed me that I have a place in the middle of your heart.
We are two people who have one dream.
We are two people who have uniting love.

LOVE PAIN

EYES TALK

I wish our eyes could talk—then everything would be simple.
We would not have anything hidden between the two of us.
We could truly be one.
Our souls could unite as one.
Even one heart could beat for both of us.

If our eyes could talk, we could for sure live one life.
We would know everything about each other.
We could share our pain.
We would not have any secrets.
We would have real love
If just our eyes could talk.

If our eyes could talk, all our fears about life would disappear.
I would be strong—I would be confident about us.
I would know you are mine.
You would know I belong to you.
I could freely love you—you would not question my love.

If our eyes could talk, we would not have need to say anything.
We could live in love and be one.

LOVE PAIN

I KNOW

I love you with all my heart.
It may not be perfect or angelic,
But it is the best and most treasured part of me.

When you are watching me,
I feel your love inside my heart.
I feel you connect with me,
And my soul responds to you.

I feel we are one—
Two bodies, two hearts, but our souls connect as one.
We complement each other,
And we each awaken the best in each other.
This is the most special
And unique aspect of our love.

I have love with you, not lust.
I know you feel the same, but still
It is just a matter of time
Until you will betray it all
Because you can't help who you are.

LOVE PAIN

BETRAYED

I wish we met in different world,
In a world where smiles are real.
Where feelings are real.
Where we are warmed by the sun and with hugs.
Maybe then our love will not be impossible.
Maybe then you will love me forever.

You made me believe that impossible is possible.
What sadness and pain are left
From something that was once so beautiful.
Eyes which were full of stars now become empty and dull.

My love for you is the biggest sorrow of my life.
I am torn between living in the happy past
Or moving into a hard, lonely present.
Even my own heart betrayed me with loving you
And still loving you.
I put on a brave face, breathe the air, and smile each day.

I wonder what would happen if we met again?
Would I still have feelings for you as I had before?
Would I hate you?
One is for sure: the love which we had left inside me a deep wound
Which I hope might heal one day.
Still, I think that after you,
I will never be able to love anyone again.

LOVE ASHES

I will never forget the way you make me feel,
A million of purple roses falling around me.
The way you make me feel still lives inside me.
To feel your eyes on me makes millions
Of purple roses bloom all around.

I will never forget the spark in your eyes
When you look at me.
I wanted this love to be deep, from your heart.
I search your eyes,
I want to know what is behind them.

If I might have known then
That nothing could compare to the love behind your eyes.
You enjoyed with me a moment of lust, but
In your chest you had not the ability of ice to melt—
You had only a piece of concrete instead of a heart.

In the end, my dream of purple roses burned,
Turned to dark ashes,
Which filled and stayed in my heart.

LOVE PAIN

WOUNDED BIRD

Hundreds of shields
That I protected myself with—
Hundreds of shields around me,
And you broke each of them
Hundreds of questions started to fly through the air
Between the two of us.

I thought about:
Things I wanted to know about you,
Questions I wanted to ask you,
Words I wanted to say to you.
Everything flies through the air between the two of us

At the end, nothing had been said or asked.
You made an unprotected, wounded bird out of me.
What once was the truth now become a lie.

You were love thirsty, but you did not want to love.
It was easy for you to go away and move on.
You never believed in anything anyway.

You ruined everything
I believed about love and being in love.
You taught me not to trust.
You also made me able to live without shields.
I became strong.
I will never be a wounded bird again.

LOVE PAIN

PRICE OF LOVE

A hundred thousand tears from my eyes.
A hundred thousand tears from my heart.
A million tears my soul already realized,
And the tears are not stopping.
Tears are still there and showing the cost
Of something that once was called love.

How many tears are needed for a heart to reconcile with dead love?
How many tears are needed for dead love to be finally mourned?
How many years for the heart are needed to cease its being wrapped in black?
What will be price enough to pay for what was once called love?

How many years of my life
Must I sacrifice as the price for a year of our love?
How many years of my life must pass before I start to live again?
How many years more
For my lips to finally make a smile and realize a sound of joy?
What will be price enough to pay for what was once called love?

Our love—my curse.
Our love—poison which makes my heart suffer.
Our love which makes my soul ill.
I wish you had taken my life instead of my heart.

LOVE PAIN

LOVE RIVER

Journey of years spent, trying to make love disappear.
Trying to forget love, which rooted inside my heart.
Each year was killing a drop of love.
Each year was killing a drop of desire for its love.
While inside me was a whole river of love to be emptied.

Love, which was a black, trembling river inside of me,
Which was flowing and flowing in a sea of pain—
A waterfall of my tears was entering into this sea of pain, too,
While I was trying to empty my heart of my love.

River of love, where was your start?
Is it from the center of the heart, or is it seeded inside the mind?
Because of its power, mine must be in my blood.
I had to find your weakness in order to kill you.
It was the only way for you to die.

My mind goes far away back.
Where did my river of love start? Can you see—
See a girl in heart, body of woman.
A man next to her who saw the world and lived it all—
Who is breaking her innocent heart—
Is this a memory, or is it just a dream?

Cry, my heart; cry, my eyes.
You see where you lost your innocence.
You see far away when a man is breaking your heart,
When you were celebrating finding love,
This man gave you pain and took your heart.
Empty your tears, innocent heart.
Now you know the difference between love and lust.
You will find strength and love again!

LOVE PAIN

INCAPABLE OF LOVE

The fire of our love which burned,
Putting the whole world itself on fire—
It turned into gray ashes and filled my heart.

Gray ashes placed inside my heart
Now remind me forever
About our love which was once
Love between man and woman
As never seen before.

Your eyes, source of power,
Which you sucked from my heart—
Come back to me, and make me glow,
To become the most beautiful woman of all.

I wonder what happened with you.
In your eyes, love was so easy to disappear,
As easy as it comes.
Have you been awakened from a dream?
Maybe for you our love never was real?

In the deep, secret and sacred space of my heart,
Which I try to hide and not to admit (not even to my own mind),
For me, our love will always burn and be real.

However, ashes are there, too.
I suppose at the end, we both chose to part.
I just wonder, was the share of our love fair?
Ashes for me and happy memories for you?

How, after this, am I to believe or fall in love ever again?

In life, love has a price just like everything else. Be sure you can afford it, and before anything else, be sure it is the right one for you.

LOVE PAIN

DISAPPEAR WITH TIME

Leaving you behind, leaving love, I thought I'd finally found.
Leaving the man who changed my life, leaving my past behind.
Leaving the life I lived and the only one I knew.
Walking forward and saying goodbye
To everything I lived for, everything I knew and had known!

Walking forward with dry eyes while my heart cried and screamed.
Walking forward straight as an arrow
While every atom of my body was broken.
I walked bravely inside darkness and pain,
Paying the price for letting myself fall in love with you.

I stayed blind after you, just as I was blind while loving you.
While my past was destroyed, my future needed to be found.
All of this while I rumbled blind through darkness after leaving you!

That was my price for loving you: "Life lost while I was yet alive."

Guilty for loving you, still sorry for not fighting for love, I found
Nothing in my love for you made sense.
Nobody could understand me, neither could I understand myself.
The only thing in my love which makes sense to me was finally saying to you,
Goodbye, and moving on with my life.

LIFE POEMS

LIFE POEMS

THE MOMENT

What happened when humanity was born?
What at this majestic moment of time happened to the world?
Did the sky open, and God acknowledged a soul
Who would live and walk in the world?

Is destiny already written up in the blue sky or between the stars?
Is destiny written already for the life of someone just born,
For someone not yet aware of the world or of what it is to be alive?
Is there already a path chosen for each person to walk?

Does it matter if there's rain and thunder or a sunny day full of golden rays?
In this special and destined moment of time
Does it matter whether the night is full of stars or a full-dark night?
Does it matter for the destiny of someone being born
What kind of day or night there is to welcome them at birth?

What happens when a soul takes air and gets to live?
Did heaven sing or hell scream?
Is it night or day, and does it matter
When soul takes air and starts to live?
What might night or day predict for the life a person will lead?

Did, at this night or day, life straightaway
Spray destiny on the newborn?
Did the soul feel tears and harden, waiting for her,
So it starts to cry?
Or maybe she looks forward to walking through the world,
So it screams, welcoming its life being born.

Is there meaning to be
Of our life once when we get born?
Once when we take air and start to cry,
Is our life already decided for us?

LIFE POEMS

FLOWER FIELDS

I am a princess from far-away wildflower fields.
I go everywhere: universe, space, cities, and villages,
But my heart always stays inside my flower fields.

I come back to my flower fields
Because nowhere else exists beauty to equal here,
Because home is where the heart lives.
I keep hidden from the world my flower fields.

I will always live there.
Even when I die, my soul will continue to be there.
My colorful flower fields, the magic that feeds my heart.
Flower fields spark magic in my heart.

LIBERO

I want to be free.
I want to be a wildflower.
I want to feed butterflies in wild fields.

I want to be a wildflower in open fields.
I want to blossom each season—
Each season I want my petals to change colors.

I want to be red in winter, blue in summer,
Green in spring, and yellow in autumn.

I want to be a rainbow flower
With leaves that are forever green.
I want my soul to be forever free.

PURPLE ROSE

I am a purple rose with petals made of love.
Sun makes golden rays for bees to find my pollen.
I am a purple rose with petals nourished by dew.
Night hides the moon to make dark for the stars
to come and make me spark.

I am a butterfly with wings full of rainbow colors.
Flowers grow for me to complement fields in green.
I am a butterfly who lives just in seasons of spring.
Flowers take colors from me to enchant the fields.

I am a soul who wants to live free in flower fields.
I am a girl who makes her own fairy tales and dreams.
Flower fields forever belong to me.
I am a woman, but still I am a shadow of this girl.

Time can pass, but our dreams and the essence of us,
Which makes us who we are, will never change.

GROWN UP

My dreams are colorful rainbows in the sky.
Rainbows which stripe the sky in beautiful colors.
My dreams are sparkling stars from the night sky.
Sparkling stars all colors and shapes
My dreams have been.

Dreams which I accumulated inside my heart
To make my life to be full of colors,
To make my days and nights
Full of sparks.

My dreams, locked inside my heart,
I had a world of my own.
I had a heaven of my own.
In my dreams, I was star at night and butterfly by day.
My dreams help me to survive life's storms.

Once heart is unlocked
All my dreams fly away, one by one.
I lost my heaven, world of my own.
I suppose this is how innocence was lost too.

I wanted to believe that dreams are forever,
But the only certainty in life of which we can be sure is
The fact that we will all die once.
I suppose I am a grown-up woman now
I can live instead of dream.

SWAN

It is my beauty that is my curse.
When my face shines my heart cries.
Everyone says it is okay for me to cry
Because I am beautiful.

It is my strength that is my curse.
When my bones are broken
My body still stands strong.
Everyone says it is okay to break me
Because I am strong.

It is my heart that is my curse.
When I love everyone, nobody loves me back.
Everyone says it is okay because I have
Enough of love already.

It is my life that is cursed.
I was a little black duckling everyone knocked in the head.
My head healed, but my heart is damaged.
I am a crying swan!

SWAN 2

White crying swan am I.
As an adult, I made my own choice to be.
I want my tears to get out.
When my heart cannot love,
At least I let it cry.

Still, nobody sees my tears.
Everyone sees the sparkling star on my head.
I stopped to be kicked,
And everyone wants to rip me.

At night
I feel like I am the only living creature who breathes air,
But it is okay.
I made my own choice to be,
To stop kicking and ripping.

My body is full of pain,
But it is okay.
My pain taught me to be proud of my star
And to keep it hard.

LOST

My forest, big, dark, and green
You are my only home.
When I am with you, I feel darkness of soul,
But still you gift me with peace.

My forest green,
You relax me and make my heart calm.
I feel I belong and blend well in this
Your dark, deep darkness green.

Am I wild?
Am I lost?
Am I just one leaf from this, your tall tree?
I wonder my forest, deep, dark, green?

Do you hear my cry and scream?
I want to know; I want to find out who am I?
Is the answer hidden in this mysterious shade of deep green?
Deep forest green, please talk to me.

I can sense a river at the end of your mysterious green.
I wonder, does this river wait for me to take me inside its flow?
I am ready to live what destiny decides for me.
Deep forest green, you are only place I ever felt at home.

Please make me see the world I am in.
While I am wandering inside your dark green
Clear your paths for me.
You are my home, but I do not belong inside you either.
I am lost wherever I go.

LIFE WIDOW

There is a woman with beautiful face and grace,
But inside she is scarred.
She is holding a rupture as big as a cannon,
Which is a reflection of her life.

Many cuts and cracks are inside her;
Still she stands straight and brave.
This is how she continues to hold her grace and to keep
Her body from falling apart.

Cuts and cracks,
The consequences of her life—
Everybody swore to her their love.
They said how special she is.
Then slowly and purposely, they cracked and damaged her.

Your beauty and grace are not fair, they said.

What is beauty and grace without love?
Without love there is no life.
You never loved me, she finally said.
Black widow I will be then and mourn my life.

BLACK ROSE

I opened my eyes inside darkness:
I heard the bells of hell and felt my soul burn.
I am inside a deep black well!
Black, black, black—no light!

Am I still sleeping?
Is this what explains why I am in the well?
Do I face evil deeds?
Am I a desperate sinner?

I closed and opened my eyes.
It was not a dream—the darkness was real.
I felt my soul go up into my heart.

I faced the demon dark, and I said:
I am not scared.
Burn my soul, and burn my heart.
From my beautiful ashes, black roses will come!

DEATH

I saw death, and I am scared!
It was a black caftan, wrapped.
I saw and witnessed that death could fly!

I thought about my soul, I wanted to cry.
Why was death above my head in flight?
I thought maybe judgment and the last day had come.
I thought about the evils of darkness, about angels from the sky.
Then I opened my eyes.

I remember my dark nights.
My prayers for a happy day.
I was ready to die for it, how unhappy my life is!
I opened my eyes and said in my mind:

No big deal!
Maybe it is just my time to die.

LIFE POEMS

PURGATORY

My body is weightless.
My soul walks through darkness, lost in a deep, black well.
I see how she struggles in the dark.

While my body is hollowed,
Pain in me is inexplicable and unbearable.
It rises each moment.
It owns and rules what is left of me.

While I am trying to manage the pain,
I look at my wrist; I want to cut myself and bleed.
I want to help myself and let pain out from my body.

While everything around is full of color,
I see only black and white.
I am looking how slowly all white color turns gray.

I start seeing only black.
I finally cut myself to bleed.
Red liquid bursts from my wrist.

I am desperate.
Enormous power of pain splits me.
My soul wanders in a cemetery with the dead.
My body, a shell, still acts as if I am alive.

I am between the world of the dead and the world of those who are alive.
O my God, what have you done to me?

When you enter into the labyrinth of darkness, faith is the only thing that can save you. If you did not already have faith, it is time to find it.

LIFE POEMS

SUFFERER

My dark night,
I am lost in the labyrinth of life.
In life where it is never day, and fog forever hides the sun
To confuse me, not to find exit, in light.

What kind of life is mine?
What kind of destiny is mine?
If I kill myself, will I kill my nightmares too?
Should I take a chance,
Choose my own destiny, or dead already am I?

What am I to do?
Why are dead souls speaking to me in the dark?
Why does nobody give me a hand to take me into the light?
Everybody knows how lost I am.

O my mother, can't you at least
Hear, from far away at night, my loud screams?
Can't you feel my deep soul sorrow, desperation, and fear?
I questioned whether you are my mother, so you left me there.

Here I cease to fear; I stop screaming.
I become numb to life inside the dark.
Love died for me, too,
Because I am left alive in a cemetery of the dead!
Now I stand straight to walk whatever path opens to me.
I do not want to hear in my life ever again,
"I love you," because love died for me too.
It stays behind me in a cemetery with the dead.

At some point of our living it can be so dark that we lose faith.
However, if we want to continue to live and have inner peace, faith must be found again.

SURVIVOR

O my mother hell, you who are holding my hand,
You who show me the difference between good and bad,
You who taught me to recognize evil and good,
You who took me in your arms and made me strong,

You are the only mother I acknowledge.
Earth mother sacrificed and abandoned me.
You accepted me and made me to be strong.
You made me to become a daughter of yours.

I kneel in front of you.
You are protecting me from the one whom you wait
To burn in your barrel of fire.
You were the only one who opened the door for me
When I was abandoned and hurt.

When I die, I do not want my soul to go to paradise.
I will never forget what I survived.
When I die, I gift you with my body and soul.
Burn it to ashes; then spread it with wind.
I honor you, my mother; you made me live my life strong.
You are my only mother, my mother hell.

LIFE POEMS

CHAINED

Chained and tied up with the past, with secrets.
Chained for days without sun and nights without stars.
Chained with invisible strings of emotion and sadness.
Chains that first tightened in me in my childhood,
They became stronger and stronger, restricting my life.

During my life I became accustomed to living with strings.
I got used to never being free.
The older I was, the heavier and stronger the strings, so
I walked stronger and harder
Until I slowly started to break my inner me.

Still I smile, laugh, and let my eyes spark.
I want to be like everybody else.
While millions of tears are accumulating inside me
I keep my eyes dry and stand brave.
I walk straight and proud like life is easy and owned by me
While my soul screams and stops wanting to live.

Being used by others becomes the strongest chain.
I become full of sadness
 Loneliness—without any dignity left in my heart.
Everybody moves in front of me, admires how capable and brave I am.
While in the night I pray to God for a moment of peace and relief
I am ready to die for it.

ANGEL TEARS

Open the heavens
Maybe out behind the beautiful blue sky.
I stare often and imagine my salvation from there.
If I am right, open the sky, please, let it rain, angels' tears to fly.

Please make a storm and thunder powerful enough to
Wash my deep pain and heal my bleeding heart.
Heal me rain from the high-above sky,
Heal my wounded heart and make it stop crying,
Wash the years of pain,
Heal the heart-scars,
Stop my mourning,
I know how powerful you are!

Please allow me to feel the sun's warmth again.
Allow me to see how stars at night shine.
Make me believe that magic exists.
Is this too much to ask?

Please, rain of life, with your thunder strong
Rip off the black caftan wrapped around my soul and my heart!

Please angels, take life's burdens from my shoulders,
Everything has to end somewhere and sometime.
Let my pain end too.
It is time for someone to hear my plea, my prayer.
My voice has power and strength, so I pray.
I am sure it reaches high up to the sky.
If God exists, he will be there and hear my prayer.
He is going to heal my heart, and I will feel love again.

MYSTIC RIVER

My life is flowing and disappearing.
My dreams are flowing and disappearing.

My life is like a piece of wood which flows in a mystic river.
It is going somewhere far—who knows where?
A piece of wood, slowly disappearing along
The flow of this green river.

Rarely is this river of my own water clear.
Rarely is there a reflection of sun spark in this river.
Just as in my life—rarely is something clear, and
There is rarely a spark of light.

Mystic river, full of dangerous swirls that
This piece of wood is caught in.
Just as in my life, I am caught in dangerous swirls all the time.
To survive and not to drown
I hold my breath in and stop breathing for a while.
When I am finally out, and everything starts to be normal,
I slowly start to breathe again.

My life is a piece of wood inside a dangerous green river,
Which I call the mystic river.
I do not understand how I am not crushed and destroyed.
It does not make sense, then, that I am destined to
Enter into the ocean and disappear there.

My sense of longing and belonging is constant.
My tears are streaming all the time along my face.
I wish to stand again at this place next to the river where I started with flow
To remind myself of
When I was not hurt and crushed inside my heart,
To bring myself in time to
Where I believed that the river is going to bring me—
On to a beautiful place full of sparks and light.

Powerful feeling of longing and belonging
For this place of innocence
Which does not exist anymore.
However, mystic green river is still there and flowing.

SOMEWHERE

I dream about freedom to unleash myself,
For a place where sadness and pain will disappear.
I wish to find peace inside my heart and my mind
Where life's heaviness will finally disappear.

I wish to find a place where I can take a breath of air,
Close my eyes, feel alive, relieve these chains of pain.
I want to find a place where I can cry,
To let out everything that chokes my heart.

I am using the last of my strength
To hold in the screams from my soul and from my heart.
I am activating the only piece of strength left inside me
In order to survive and not die.

I am taking the last piece of strength left in me
To walk forward, to leave life-and-love wounds behind.
I want back my freedom to break invisible chains.
I want my life to be my own again.

LIFE POEMS

PRAY

Dear God, I am sorry I lost faith in you,
But still I wonder, did I ever believe
you existed and that you are real?

Still, why have I been questioning so much?
Why have I been tested so much?
Is this because you taught me about life?

I know now when I was broken and tested
In my heart, you were with me.
You are the one who helped me survive.

A woman with a crown, a queen, which everybody sees?
I am a person of flesh and blood just like everyone else,
Someone who was in search of peace
And nothing more.

This life journey of mine taught me a lot.
I am happy that I found you, and my faith was born.
I can see myself living finally in peace.

LIFE POEMS

ESSENCE OF LIFE

We live in a beautiful world of blue skies and green grass,
But sometimes it is hard to notice, to have a joy.
We need to see the beauty of nature around us, to walk on green grass,
Not to ignore the essence of the world that makes joy.

If we close our eyes, it is easy to find what the heart is meant to love.
The delusions of our mind we should forget.
Clearing our mind, our hearts will love the essence of life.
Deep inside ourselves, we will know what is the right way to live.

Flowers are meant to be seen, but they enchant us with their smell.
When we reach the end of the street, it does not have to be the end.
An eternal sky is proof that the end can't be reached.
God is the only one who knows where everything starts and finishes.
He made the world to be enjoyed—it is up to us to take joy.

RAIN

Love the rain.
When it's raining,
 all walls around me stop tightening and lose strength.
It feels like life finally stops and drowns in a moment of silence.
Everything becomes quiet.
Life pressures disappear, and pain washes away.

Love the rain.
When it's raining,
I close my eyes, and I can feel rain drops on my skin.
It brings me back to the time when I was a child.
When rain was warm, and I was barefoot,
I would run outside and walk through mud.
It brings me back to the time when I needed just a little bit to be happy.

Love the rain.
I can cry,
 and my tears can be rain drops too.
I can let myself be weak and live in harmony with the rain.
I will not feel guilt then for being weak.
Rain is magic; it makes flowers to bloom and grass to grow.
If you would be with me, rainy days would be the most beautiful days.

LION KING

Have a lion heart.
Hunt; do not be hunted.
Drink blood if you must.
Do not let other drink yours.

Be fast, be sharp, be strong!

Live like a lion.
Do not depend on others.
Be above the world not under.
Be a lion—be a king.

Do not live in fear like a mouse!
Live without fear like a lion king!

HERO

A hero does not have to be on a pedestal.
Nobody can stand on a pedestal for all of a life.
Sometimes people get there by pure luck.

A hero is a person who can stand straight and proudly on a pedestal.
They walk with dignity and stay true to themselves
While walking through the hardest parts of life.
Vice versa

When experiencing life pain and failure
It is important that they stay true to themselves.
People who can do this—they are the true heroes.
They stand on life's pedestal, not on an artificial one.

QUEEN

I am a queen without crown.
I do not need one to prove it and show who am I!

When I do not have a dress of silk
The sun dresses me up all in gold.
There are hundreds of shining stars around me
Which follow me when I walk.

Everybody sees this and bows in front of me because
I have a mind like a queen.
I walk like a queen.
I talk like a queen.
I smile like a queen.
I am generous like a queen.
I punish like a queen,
And I cry like a queen, too.

I love as a woman, but
Only a true king can stand next to me.
Any other man would feel like a crab.

I am a woman.
I am a queen.

LIFE POEMS

CHILDREN OF GOD (collaborative poetry)

by Tobi Marho

Valiant in mind, heart in despair.
I can not fight.
Set aside your disbelief.
I will stand by your side
in your unbelief.

And then I wake again,
To the brunt of sneering sun.
Spiriting past the blinds.
Spiriting towards my space.
Steeling the darkness.

My darkness preserves in my faith.
My darkness, ensuring my sanity.
My darkness worships my disbelief.
My darkness becomes my life.

My friend you found me,
While I am living in darkness.
Still I will stand next to you
But I am unbeliever.
I do not believe there is life
dark or chains free.

LIFE POEMS

By Stacy Nicholson

Peace in mind, warrior in heart.
I am a believer, fire burns in me.
For freedom I will fight.

I will stand next to you my friend.
I will fight for you, too.
My shadow will protect you from brunt,
For you to experience light and not to burn.

Believer or disbeliever,
in our essence we are the same.
We rise and fall and get tested all.
When our hearts connect
They will beat as one.
You will get light and you will start to believe.

I hear your screams from the dark.
You listen , you will hear my calls from light.
Take my hand, we will walk
to find horizon together.

Today I hold your hand my friend.
Tomorrow when I fall you will hold mine.
We stick together as one to reach
and live under the sun.

WE ARE ALL CHILDREN OF GOD.

LIFE POEMS

Children of God

Authors:

Tobi Marho, Nigeria
Stacy Nicholson, Australia.

FANTASY POEMS

FANTASY POEMS

PLAYFUL FAIRY

Once upon a time,
Between the stars and under the moon,
I flew at night.
I made rainbow magic in the dark.

You saw me.
You found me while I was hiding
Under an eternity of sky.

I wanted to know who you are.
What magic did you have? How did you find me?

You squeezed inside a ray of light with me.
You changed a lonely place under the stars
Into a perfect dream.

You said to me:
"Dragon, am I."
I spread the wings, you burned them.
Tears ran down my face.
I said:
"You are human, and I am the dream you destroyed."

FANTASY POEMS

MODERN FAIRY TALE

It is spring, the forest is beautiful and green.
A young deer escaped from its mother to play
 In the sun which finally welcomes a season of green.

In the grass are colorful butterflies who fly
And rainbow flowers who are excited
To warm leaves and petals under the spring sun.

They all welcome the deer and join in play
To have fun and enjoy life.

It is the season of the hunt.
An old hunter walks through the forest,
When he spots this beautiful view, a picture of glorious play.

He stalks from the corner
While sharpening his arrow
And aiming—eyes on the deer.

The deer stops and meets hunter's eyes.
Hunter stands and lets arrow fly.
He said: what glorious prey.
I found an innocent heart, and now it is mine.
What a capable hunter am I.

FANTASY POEMS

PRINCESS FROM THE DARK

I am born from the stars.
Grown up through darkness'
I walked heavy steps through hell.
Then I took the sword and
Raised myself in light!

My heart is from the stars,
But my power is from the dark.
Angels thought me to suffer.
Hell thought me to rise and
Give me strength to
Take life over and survive.

FANTASY POEMS

POWER OF HEART

My mother is a burning fire of power.
My father is strength and carriage.
I grew up in the forest and nature fields.
I grew up in green grass, picking wildflowers.

In my heart is the power of burning light.
In my blood runs an ocean of darkness.
My mind is a mountain.

I am a loner.
I am carrying the sword with both of my hands.
I slay the dragons in the air and conquer the word.

I am a mixture of black and white,
Mixture of dark and light, mixture of sun and moon.
I am a woman who is born with
Power and thunder in her heart.

FANTASY POEMS

WARRIOR PRINCESS

I had been born as a beautiful dreamer.
When I grew up, my earth mother sacrificed me to God.
In order for her sins to be washed,
She honored my sister's lives

Hell spread its hands and accepted what my earth mother sent.
Hell wrapped me up and said:
"I am your mother now. I am your father now."

My innocence did what my mother wanted me to do.
I honoured my mother's wish and let my soul go.
I honored my mother, and I served with my hands and with my heart.

In the dark, I never close my eyes.
I felt burning and pain in my soul.
Hell washed my soul and lifted me up to the sky.
Angels gave me a new heart.
Instead of a dreamer, I became a warrior.

I walk under the sun and sleep under the moon.
I am made from the ashes of a dreamer.
Hell is my mother, angels my godmothers.
My new parents will hold me forever.
What God decides, humans can't change.
Warrior Princess am I.

FANTASY POEMS

MULTIPLIED

I am one woman who lives two lives,
Day life and night life.
I am one woman with many faces.
I am one woman with many personalities.

During the day I carry sword and heavy shield.
I run, fight, hunt, and kill.
I like and enjoy using my strength, power, and carriage.
I am a fighter and a warrior.

During the night, I am a beautiful woman.
I wear silk, lace, and diamonds.
I like and enjoy mind manipulation and domination.
I seduce and enslave.

I am a woman with one hundred faces.
I like and nourish each of them.
They are all part of me and make me unique.
I am a loner.

I do not belong to anyone, and I do not want
Anyone to belong to me.
God is the only one who has power above me.
I bend and kneel only in front of him
Because he is the one who made me.

WOMAN LOVE

LOVE INTIMACY

Look inside my eyes.
You will see inside my soul.
You will see inside my heart.

Look inside my eyes.
You will see my father and my mother.
You will see my life,
My fall and my rise.

Look inside my eyes.
You will see a secret
Which I hide.

WOMAN LOVE

SILENCE

I love your silence.
It makes you different from everybody else.
I love your trembling when you kiss me.
It makes all the world's pain disappear.

You are like nobody else.
When my mind wants to fight you,
My heart tells me how stupid I am
For trying to do battle with you,
Which never existed.

I wish you would teach me about love
Because I only know pain.
I love your silence the most about you.

WOMAN LOVE

WOMAN KNOWS

I do not care which kind of love wind you are
Because you are one who is meant to blow for me.
I will go anywhere in the world for you.

I do not care if our love is poisonous or sweet,
I will eat it anyway.
If it is sweet, I will share it with you,
and if it is poison, I will swallow it as well,
As long as you prepare to die with me.

You are my sailor who sails over the deep sea.
I am a siren, and I sing love songs for you.
I want to love you, but if you do not let me,
I will kill you.

I sing for you—surrender to me, and let me love you.
I sing for you, and magic is released!

WOMAN LOVE

LOVE LETTER

My beloved one, when I am waiting for you to come,
Your love is a flame in my heart which lights my life.

I hope my love—
Silk and velvet I placed in your heart—
Will warm you on cold nights.

We are two drops of love
Which merge into an ocean of life.
Instead of disappearing inside this ocean,
Our love makes the ocean of life disappear,
And infinity becomes ours.

Two of us, two mortals
Who have the power of the ocean inside—
Because of this power, these strengths,
And light—all made by our love—

We will disappear.
Our ashes will be carried by the wind one day,
But our love will be written about and live on forever.

WOMAN LOVE

HIDDEN INSIDE OCEAN

You are my ocean of power
Swallowing me with lust and desire.
I am a drop of golden love flame
Burning and living inside your heart.

You are my dark ocean
Which carries dangerous waves and storms.
Waves and storms I enjoy moving and provoking.

I am your strength and desire.
Every time you look at me
I make your heart beat and feel that you want to live.

With you I am sun and moon.
I assure you I always have lightning in life.
You assure me there is always reason for me to shine.
This is how our love functions to make us live and breathe.

LIFE IS NOT A CUP OF COFFEE

Close your eyes, and you will hear my whisper.
Close your eyes, and you will hear my call.
Close your eyes, and you will feel my touch.
You will feel my kiss.

I want you to love me now in this life
Because I do not believe in any other.
I do not want your words and then your hand to touch.
I want to look you in your eyes when you kiss me.

I am not a girl to listen about stars.
I am a woman, and I want a man to hold me.
Close your eyes, and listen to my whispers.
Come to me—I want to love and be loved.

BLUE LIGHT TANGO

Look inside my eyes.
Connect with me.
I want to dance a tango of love with you.

I want to dance with you
Under blue light.
I want to feel with you a
Universe of love.

Make a delightful vibration inside me
And let the dance begin.

Dance with me this tango of love
Under blue light.

WOMAN LOVE

FLOWER

Your eyes are turning me into a flower.
I feel
I am growing.
I am blooming.

Your eyes make me feel
I am lying in soft rose petals.
Then I feel your eyes start slowly to move
All these petals, all over my body.

Your eyes—intensity—
I feel their touch all over my body,
And when they are touching me
I pray they never stop.

While you see beauty in me,
I see power in you.

WOMAN LOVE

FLOWER 2

You see an angel.
I see a power that needs tasting.
I will move rose petals you covered me with.
I will stand in front of you.

You want me?
You will have to prove your power.

I will laugh at you.
I will show you everything I have,
but you will not be allowed to touch anything.
I will taste your control.
I will make you jealous.
To taste the power of your mind
When you explode, and your eyes
start shifting through all the rainbow colors,
I will be angel again
Just to play you all over again from the start!

Then I will become devil again.
I will expose my sex desire.
I will walk you through fire to see if you can follow me.
I will walk you through dark tunnels full of devils to taste your fears.

If you want me, you must have more power than I do.
You will have to make each woman in me surrender.
I am multiplied!

WOMAN LOVE

SINNER

I like your powerful darkness.
It is irresistible—when you look at me
The fire in your eyes makes my blood boil.

I want to test my woman-strength on you.

I want to use my femininity
To burn you to ashes.
You made me into a black devil.
Everything that was innocent in my heart
Died when our eyes met.

WOMAN LOVE

IN ACTION

I am woman, swirl of fire and power.
My eyes make mystery and intrigue.

You can't pass next to me because my scent is irresistible.
I am power, excitement, which everyone wants to taste,
So you also will want to.

Nothing around me can sleep, and neither will you.
I will make your night restless from now on to forever.

I will be brought to you in black love to make a sin of you,
To prove my power and have fun with you.

WOMAN LOVE

BLACK LOVE

Darkness but magic—magic but black magic.
Opium and euphoria abound,
All tempting, all forbidden.
Black love at its best!

What would you do
If forbidden garden of black love opened the door for you?

Would you enter inside,
Lie between beautiful, dark red roses of passion,
Cover yourself with its petals?
Would you enter inside, close your eyes,
Take joy of euphoria and breathe opium?

What would you sacrifice
For a taste of a magic, black love?
What would you give for a heart to be wrapped
In swirls of golden love dust and shining stars:
Innocence, years of life, your whole life or even your soul?

Once you get inside it, you've sacrificed everything already.
Take what you can while it lasts
It is just a matter of time until you will pay the price!

WOMAN LOVE

PLAYFUL

I look at you,
Walk with and smile on you,
To make you dream about me.

I dress to make you sweat.
I want you to sense beauty underneath my clothing.
I want your body to shake in desire,
To connect and explore me.

I want you to obsess over me.
I already see in your reflection the way I make you feel.

I see in your eyes desire,
Thirst for love, thirst for lust too—
Your attempts to hide it all failing.

Your eyes speak truth to me.
I want to kill any prejudice you have about love.
I want you to cover me like a blanket
With your love and passion.

My heart and mind want
To get a taste of love with you.
I want to surrender to you.
I do not want to waste the gifts of love
Life put in front of me.

WOMAN LOVE

SEDUCTION

I cannot stop looking into his eyes.
I am so excited by his love obsession.

All my blood is boiling.
I become predator.

My eyes let him know where he stands.
My body plays the game, touch me if you can.
My smile lets him know what I am doing.

His obsession is on another level.
He can't control himself.
His soul becomes my possession!

WOMAN LOVE

DOMINATION

Your real world is fantasy.
I will make this fantasy of yours real.
I am getting into your universe to play.
I will crash all your shining stars
and turn them into grains of sand.

You will be earth, and I will be air.
You will grow flowers for me.
I will make a breeze and play with it.
Then I will make a tornado and
Spin you in all directions.

In your universe with snow and angels
I will bring black magic and make ice of you.
Then you will be crushed but not melted.
I will give you real and burning love,
Not a fantasy.

WOMAN LOVE

ONLY ONE

I want to dance for you
In the dark night full of arrows of love-light.
I want to be your dancer
And make love inside your heart.
I want your heart to tremble and live
As I dictate and give charge how to beat.

I want to dance for you
When the sun showers me with millions of light rays.
I want to be diamond sparks inside your dark eyes.
I want to blind you, so you can't see
Anything but me.

I will dance for you—
Dance of black mystery or magic of seductive love—
I do not care which one.
I want to blind you and enchant you.
In my heart nothing exists but you.
I will do anything a woman can do
To make you love me and be the only one for you.

WOMAN LOVE

LOVE ENCHANTMENT

Your love,
Millions of white snowflakes falling from sky,
Making me into a white angel and giving me wings to fly—
White snowflakes, melting inside love dreams.

Our love,
Swirl of love snowflakes, which fly around our hearts—
Your eyes gaze my blanket of silk, which falls and moves all over me.
Your eyes make love with me while my eyes shoot sparks
From the burning fire of my heart.

I am walking toward you with closed eyes,
Following a path of love you are sparking with shining stars.
I am following my heart to drown in your arms.
Your love, my angel wings, my heart beats.
Our love—mystery in the air created between us.

WOMAN LOVE

LUST DESIRE

Blind my eyes, love me.
I want to feel lust.

Make this excitement to rule inside my body!

Give me the joy of lust spreading through my veins.
Make my body shake
When lust starts spreading through my veins inside my blood.

I want lust to take me over.
Blind my eyes and love me—let our love burst into lust.

Give me the pleasure of excitement.
Make mystery touches all over me.
I want the electricity of lust flashing to cut the darkness.
Make my body shake—make it cry for your touch.

Make me happy.
Blind my eyes and make love with me.
Give me a mysterious love full of lust.
I want our love to burst into lust.

WOMAN LOVE

SEX DESIRE

If I were made of ice,
You would melt me into warm water
With only a look, the power of your eyes.
If I were a stone statue, you would cause me to crumble, pale sand pit
From the splash of your desire.

You stir in me everything that can be stirred.
From blood to brain, you provoke me so.
If I were ocean and you mountain,
I would swallow you into my deepest darkness.
No matter how high your heights, I would reach.
If I were ocean,
The world would be flooded with my waves.

You are leaving me with nothing else
But a heart beating inside my chest.
Everything else in me betrayed me,
Disappeared to become yours
While pleading with you to take it and connect.

If I had never heard the word for love,
Now I would know what it is:
Feelings of desire, lust, obsession, connection.
Wishes to completely surrender—two becoming one.
The feelings somebody stirs in you have become
Unstoppable and uncontrollable.

WOMAN LOVE

MAN POWER

Satisfy the fire in me which you lit.
I can't control the fire anymore.
Save me from the burning.

Your eyes make love wounds all over me.
Stop burning—start healing me.
My body is disappearing under your look.

Love me, desire will kill me.
Breathe in my mouth, inhale the life inside me.
You are making me to shrink in a bowl of pain
Which continues to shrink.

I am setting on fire everything around me.
You are turning me into ashes.
Have mercy and take me.
Fire is uncontrollable—help me!

WOMAN LOVE

BLACK STORM

What do you see in my eyes?

Do you see azure diamonds from a dark blue sky?
Do you see the fire I am making around me?
Do you see the mysterious woman I hide?
Do you see the life you want in me?

What do my eyes make you feel?

Is it excitement—lust—which makes your body tremble and shake?
Is it desire to enter inside my world, my dream?
Is it happiness because you found me a woman?
Is it love?

When I look at you
I see your desire like fire coming from your heart.
Excitement—lust—as electricity flushes from your eyes.
Obsession with me because of how I make you feel.

I see in you a toy for playing with, you are losing your cool.
I see power, which I shake.
I see a black sky and potential thunder
Coming above me.
I see danger, which excites me!

WOMAN LOVE

MEET ME

Meet me where blue sky touches earth.
In this place of love, where happiness starts,
Follow the paths of our dreams, and you will get there.
You will find me waiting for you.

Meet me where mountains disappear in the air.
High above the world, where mystery is born,
Just walk forward and follow shadows of love.
You will find me waiting for you.

Meet me where the ocean hides the sun.
Where the most beautiful colors are made,
Sail the ocean on ships of love to meet the horizon.
You will find me waiting for you.

Meet me where our eyes will make love,
Where our hearts will smile on each other,
Where our souls will become one.
If you search, you will find me in the place of love
Where destiny decided we would be together.

WOMAN LOVE

STAR DUST

Come to me; I will be your light.
Millions of stars will sparkle for you from my eyes.
We will break the chains of life
And make love in the dark of night.

Come to me; I want to spend a night with you.
Transport us inside a passionate dream.
I will hide the bitterness of my heart
And let you kiss and taste honey from my lips.

Come to me; I will be your muse of night.
You will smell roses which grow in my mind.
I will seed love in your heart
And enchant your mind.

Come to me.
I want to make a dream of you.
In my life, nothing is real.
I am star dust blown by winds of love
Meant to lust for just one night.

WOMAN LOVE

ANGELE MINE

Stay with me, Angele mine,
Do not let go of my hand, don't let me walk alone.
You are my shining star.
Without you, where could I go?

Stay with me, Angele mine.
Without you, all flowers will dry.
Without you, roses will not bloom.
With you, all beauty comes alive.
Keep the enchantment of my life alive.

Stay with me, Angele mine,
While I dream about you, make it last.
Keep stars at night to sparkle.
Without you, they will hide.
They will not shine.

Stay with me, Angele mine.
My swirl of love who enchanted
My soul and my heart, do not leave me.
Without you, my heart could not beat.
My blood would become a river dry.
You are my enchantment, my second half.

WOMAN LOVE

WHAT A WOMAN WANTS

What does a woman want?
Her mind to connect,
Her body to be loved and touched—
This is what every woman wants.

What does a woman want?
Her heart to feel alive and to
Burn in fire from desire—
A pleasurable torture that activates the senses,
A man who is strong and who
Will challenge her to surrender—
This is what every woman wants.

What does a woman want?
She wants to follow her heart.
She wants to give her heart what it asks for—
This is what every woman wants.

What does a woman want?
When man's desire for her is activated
And starts pulling her forward—
Her strength to lose the battle—
This is what every woman wants.

What does a woman want?
She wants to be chased by a man
And by this man to be caught.
A woman wants this man to adapt
And to play the game by her rules.

A woman wants to be for a man the one.
This is what every woman wants!

WOMAN LOVE

ONE WITH WINGS

Desire of mine,
Who is listening now at night to your heart
With head gently falling on your chest?
Who do you wrap now in silky blanket of love?
Did you forget the picture of our souls' dance, an eternity of love?

Desire of mine,
Far away across the ocean and many mountains high,
What did you do with our love, desire of mine?
Did you bury it in soil black and put a cross over it,
Or did you feed wildflowers in green fields?
What did you do with our love, desire of mine?

Desire of mine,
Was I your life love or your burning flame of lust?
Did I own your heart or mind?
What did your black heart desire of my heart?
Instead of celebrating our love, it made it die.

Now, goodbye my love.
I will blow pieces of our love from my heart into the wind
To be spread on all sides of the world.
Goodbye love of my life, love of my soul and heart.
I release my love to disappear inside the winds of life
And to continue through the air to feed young lovers' hearts.

WOMAN LOVE

LOVE?

Perfect love is just love which
Parents have for a child, or spiritual love.

Adult love is anything but perfect.
Often people are enchanted with each other
Because they are so different—
They are tempted to sin, to ruin purity.

Even if it does not go so far, still it rules—
Obsession, possession, jealousy, fear of betrayal—

There is no perfection in love if love is real and sincere.

WHAT I BELIEVE ABOUT HUMAN EXISTENCE

Life starts and finishes with a heartbeat.

The heart is the most important and powerful organ in humans—more important than the brain. Once your heart stops working, life is finished. But when the brain stops working, if the heart is strong and passionate for life, it can activate the brain again.

Our feelings and the way the heart works make us who we are. We make connections with other humans from the feelings of our heart; we store memories in our hearts, and our happiness and sadness come from the heart, too. Our carriage in life comes from the heart. The heart makes our life what it is—sometimes sweet and sometimes bitter.

When your brain finds itself in darkness, your heart can turn on a light in your mind. But when the heart is in darkness, it is seldom possible for there to be light ever again. Anything that dies inside your heart can't be reborn. It is like a flower: once it dies, the root is finished. It will never grow again; no water or food can help.

My life was very hard, but it does not matter how much darkness there once was in my life and in my brain. The light in my heart was always burning. My heart saved me in tough times, and it made me into a person who was admired over and over for passion in life and for compassion toward others.

NAMASTE

Stacy Nicholson

ABOUT THE AUTHOR

Stacy Nicholson was born in a remote village in Bosnia, a former Yugoslavian republic. She grew up as a middle daughter of poor, hard-working farmers. Nicholson came as a refugee to Australia in 2002 where she finished a degree in Library Information Services. Nicholson worked in a number of different occupations, including the last ten years in library services. Nicholson served the City of Melbourne Library Services, the Law Library as well as several other, highly rated library services in Victoria. Working on the front lines with customers, Nicholson has served people from all walks of life.

In 2014 Nicholson experienced a powerful episode of psychosis, which lasted for two months. It took her two years to recover before she was able to step back into life, at which point Nicholson started to live life very slowly all over again.

Her writing reflects a strong passion and deep feeling for life and love. Nicholson can be described as an author for new generations because she deals with the issues faced by today's generation: raw feelings about love, sex, desire, fantasy, dreaming, and suffering. Nicholson's writing is characterized by a strong sense power, and it carries positive messages about both life and love. Her most popular poems celebrate love between a man and a woman.

Nicholson has also written an autobiography, *Colour of My Heart*.

www.ingramcontent.com/pod-product-compliance
Lightning Source LLC
Chambersburg PA
CBHW060405160426
42811CB00089B/2359/J